William Bolcom

Capriccio

for
Violoncello and Piano

I. Allegro con spirito
II. Molto Allegro
III. Like a Barcarolle
IV. Gingando (Brazilian tango)
    Tombeau d'Ernesto Nazareth

Duration: *ca.* 15 minutes

Note

CAPRICCIO was commissioned by and written for the Harry Clark-Sanda Schuldmann Duo and had its premiere at The Coolidge Auditorium, The Library of Congress, Washington, D.C., on March 11, 1988.

The four-movement work is very much like a sonata in outward form, although the proportions are unusual. There is a Brahms-cum-Milhaud urge behind the piece, including the Brazilian tango at its end, in the tradition of Ernesto Nazareth.

William Bolcom

ISBN 978-0-7935-4255-0

EDWARD B. MARKS MUSIC COMPANY

EXCLUSIVELY DISTRIBUTED BY
HAL•LEONARD® CORPORATION
7777 W. BLUEMOUND RD. P.O. BOX 13819 MILWAUKEE, WI 53213

Capriccio
for Violoncello and Piano

I.

Allegro con spirito, (♩=*ca.*100); **very rhythmic**

William Bolcom
(1985)

Accidentals obtain throughout a beamed group.

For music with a key signature, traditional rules apply.

Sept. 12, 1985
Ann Arbor

II.

Molto Adagio: espressivo (♩=*ca.*50 or slower)

(The *sf*'s not too strong)

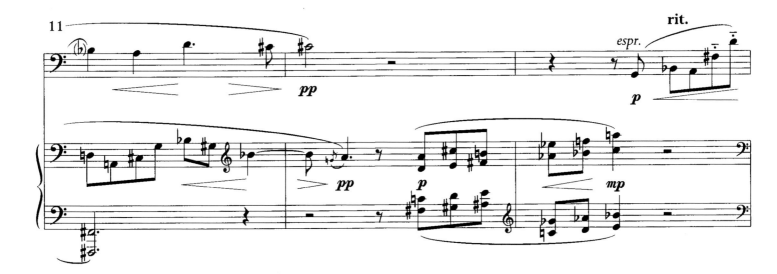

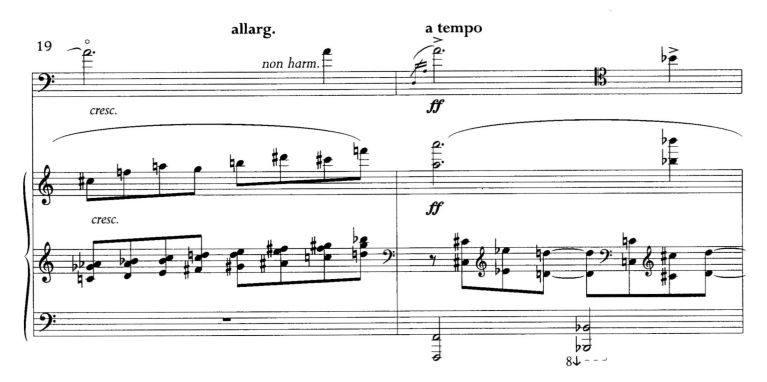

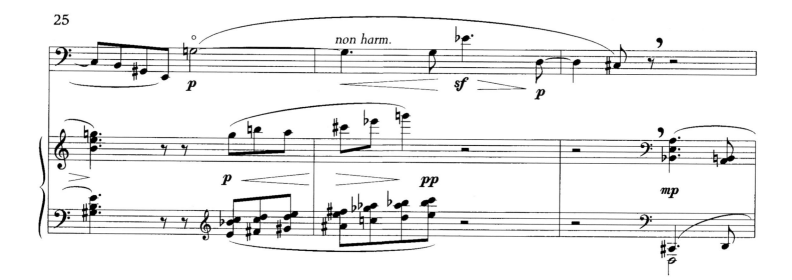

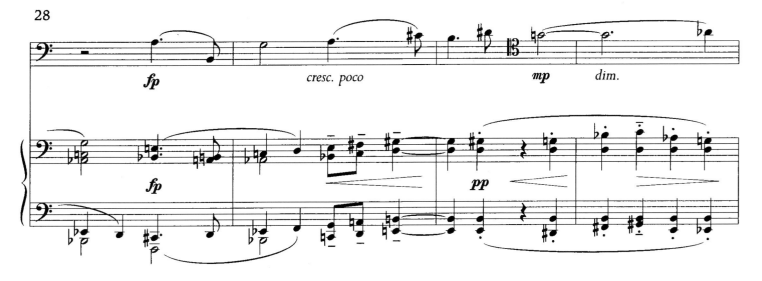

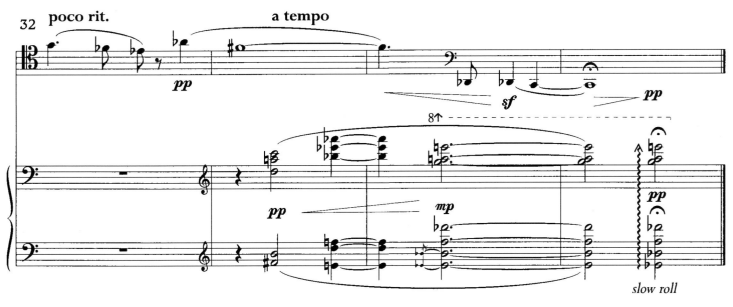

Sept. 22, 1985
Ann Arbor

III.

Like a barcarolle ($\quarternote$ = *ca.*92); tempo giusto

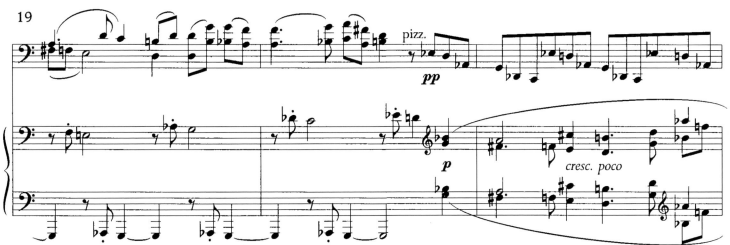

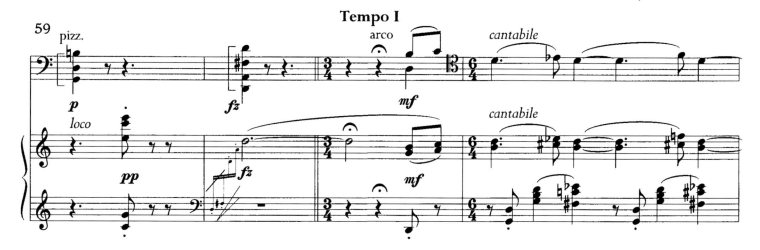

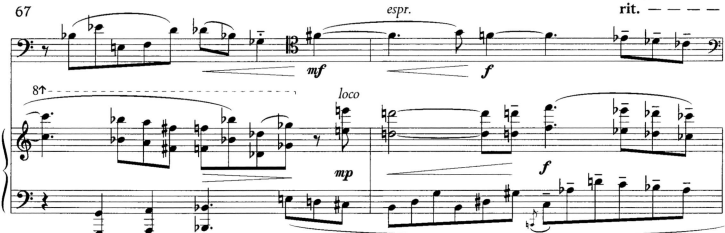

Sept. 16, 1985
Ann Arbor

IV.

Gingando - Brazilian Tango Tempo (♩ = *ca.* 80) Tombeau d'Ernesto Nazareth *

* Ernesto Nazareth (1863-1934), great composer of tangos and other dances, of Rio de Janeiro.

William Bolcom

Capriccio

for
Violoncello and Piano

I. Allegro con spirito
II. Molto Allegro
III. Like a Barcarolle
IV. Gingando (Brazilian tango)
   Tombeau d'Ernesto Nazareth

Duration: *ca.* 15 minutes

Note

CAPRICCIO was commissioned by and written for the Harry Clark-Sanda Schuldmann Duo and had its premiere at The Coolidge Auditorium, The Library of Congress, Washington, D.C., on March 11, 1988.

The four-movement work is very much like a sonata in outward form, although the proportions are unusual. There is a Brahms-cum-Milhaud urge behind the piece, including the Brazilian tango at its end, in the tradition of Ernesto Nazareth.

William Bolcom

ISBN 978-0-7935-4255-0

EXCLUSIVELY DISTRIBUTED BY

7777 W. BLUEMOUND RD. P.O. BOX 13819 MILWAUKEE, WI 53213

Capriccio
for Violoncello and Piano

Violoncello

I.

Allegro con spirito, (♩=ca.100); very rhythmic

William Bolcom
(1985)

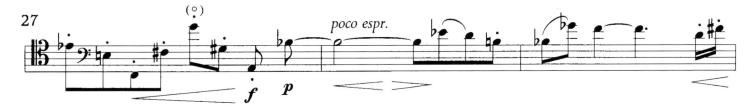

4

II.

Molto Adagio: espressivo (♩ = *ca.* **50 or slower**)

III.

Like a barcarolle ($\bullet$ = *ca.*92**); tempo giusto**

Turn Page

IV.

Gingando - Brazilian Tango Tempo (♩ = *ca.*80) Tombeau d'Ernesto Nazareth

13

114

dim.

più mosso
molto martell.

119
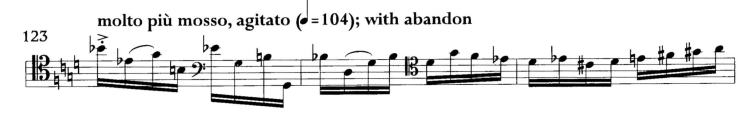

p

ff

molto più mosso, agitato ($\bullet$=104); with abandon

123

126

at heel, roughly

129

sim.

ff

133

ff

2

William Bolcom

Born in Seattle, composer/pianist WILLIAM BOLCOM entered the University of Washington at age eleven to study composition and piano. He subsequently studied composition with Darius Milhaud in California and Paris and holds degrees from the University of Washington, Mills College, the Paris Conservatoire and Stanford University. His compositions have won awards and fellowships from BMI, the Guggenheim Foundation, the Rockefeller Foundation, and the McKim Foundation, among others. His orchestral works have been performed by the Los Angeles Philharmonic, the New York Philharmonic, the Chicago, San Francisco and St. Louis symphonies, the Cologne Orchestra, the St. Paul Chamber Orchestra, and the Chamber Music Society of Lincoln Center, to mention a few.

Since 1973 Mr. Bolcom has taught composition at the University of Michigan School of Music, which in 1977 awarded him the prestigious Henry Russel Award. In 1978 and 1989 he was composer-in-residence at the Aspen Music Festival. He composed the Cello Sonata there. His "Songs of Innocence and of Experience" from the poems of William Blake were premiered at the Stuttgart Opera in January of 1984 and have since been performed in Ann Arbor, Chicago, Brooklyn, St. Louis and New York.

In 1988 Mr. Bolcom won the Pulitzer Prize in Music for his "12 New Etudes for Piano." His opera "McTeague," commissioned by the Lyric Opera of Chicago, received its world premiere October 31, 1992.

Other Bolcom works featuring the cello are "Sonata" for cello and piano, "Dark Music" for timpani and cello, "Fairy Tales" for viola, cello and contrabass, and "Fantasia Concertante" for viola, violoncello and orchestra, which had its first performance by the Vienna Philharmonic during Mozart Week in Salzburg, Austria, in 1986.

molto più mosso, agitato (♩ = 104); with abandon

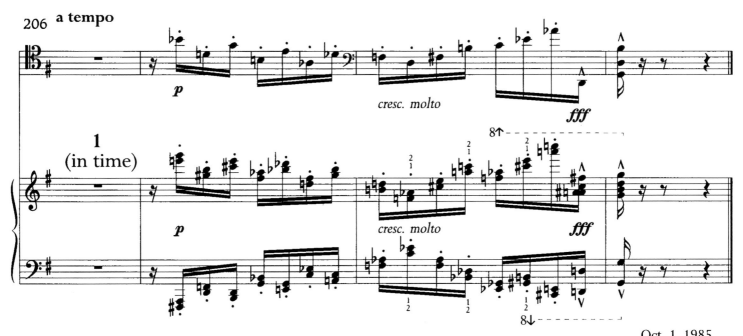

Oct. 1, 1985
Ann Arbor

William Bolcom

Born in Seattle, composer/pianist WILLIAM BOLCOM entered the University of Washington at age eleven to study composition and piano. He subsequently studied composition with Darius Milhaud in California and Paris and holds degrees from the University of Washington, Mills College, the Paris Conservatoire and Stanford University. His compositions have won awards and fellowships from BMI, the Guggenheim Foundation, the Rockefeller Foundation, and the McKim Foundation, among others. His orchestral works have been performed by the Los Angeles Philharmonic, the New York Philharmonic, the Chicago, San Francisco and St. Louis symphonies, the Cologne Orchestra, the St. Paul Chamber Orchestra, and the Chamber Music Society of Lincoln Center, to mention a few.

Since 1973 Mr. Bolcom has taught composition at the University of Michigan School of Music, which in 1977 awarded him the prestigious Henry Russel Award. In 1978 and 1989 he was composer-in-residence at the Aspen Music Festival. He composed the Cello Sonata there. His "Songs of Innocence and of Experience" from the poems of William Blake were premiered at the Stuttgart Opera in January of 1984 and have since been performed in Ann Arbor, Chicago, Brooklyn, St. Louis and New York.

In 1988 Mr. Bolcom won the Pulitzer Prize in Music for his "12 New Etudes for Piano." His opera "McTeague," commissioned by the Lyric Opera of Chicago, received its world premiere October 31, 1992.

Other Bolcom works featuring the cello are "Sonata" for cello and piano, "Dark Music" for timpani and cello, "Fairy Tales" for viola, cello and contrabass, and "Fantasia Concertante" for viola, violoncello and orchestra, which had its first performance by the Vienna Philharmonic during Mozart Week in Salzburg, Austria, in 1986.